IMAGES
of America

HICKSVILLE

Since its settlement in the 1850s, Hicksville has been a prominent Long Island transportation crossroads. In this *c.* 1980 photograph, the view is to the north from over Fourth Street. The Long Island Rail Road is crossing west to east and dividing at the right center. In the foreground, Old Country Road, also running from west to east, is bisected by three prominent north–south highways: Newbridge Road, Jerusalem Avenue, and Broadway. At the lower right is today's middle school. At the upper left is Stern's Department Store and the Mid-Island Shopping Plaza (today's Broadway Mall), one of the first regional shopping centers in the United States. The top-grossing Sears Roebuck store is in the upper right. The buildings in view represent the economic features for which Hicksville is known: numerous bank branches, medical insurance firms, and hundreds of retail and personal service establishments. (Skyview Inc.)

IMAGES
of America

HICKSVILLE

Richard E. and Anne Evers

ARCADIA

First printed in 2000.

Published by Arcadia Publishing,
an imprint of Tempus Publishing, Inc.
2 Cumberland Street
Charleston, SC 29401

Printed in Great Britain.

Library of Congress Catalog Card Number: 00-106504

For all general information contact Arcadia Publishing at:
Telephone 843-853-2070
Fax 843-853-0044
E-Mail sales@arcadiapublishing.com

For customer service and orders:
Toll-Free 1-888-313-2665

Visit us on the internet at http://www.arcadiapublishing.com

These American Legionnaires pose with packages for the U.S. Armed Forces in Vietnam. From left to right they are Richard Hochbreuckner, Russell Schubert, Bill Combe, Robert Mangels, Dick Evers, Steve Wladyka, Joe Slattery, and John Dobson. (Local History Room/HPL.)

CONTENTS

The Broadway Hotel, Hicksville, L. I.

The Broadway Hotel was erected by Frank Reinhardt *c.* 1900; it was located on Broadway at East Cherry Street. It served later as the site of Schwartz Furniture Store, which was succeeded by Phillips Silk Flowers Company.

ACKNOWLEDGMENTS

Hicksville is fortunate to have community organizations and individuals who work to preserve the memories and incidents of the village's earlier life and its contemporary evolution. The pictorial collections of the Hicksville Public Library (HPL) and the Hicksville Gregory Museum (HGM) are rich in old and current photographs. Fine photocopies from the Nassau County Historical Museum collection are included through the courtesy of County Historian Edward Smits.

Skilled photographer Edward Bady, who has copied many hundreds of Hicksville pictures, is represented, as is Harold Kelly, whose camera lens preserved so many now-gone buildings in his new 1950s community. Always interested in this project has been Bill Clark, native son, a photo historian and a popular columnist of "Jottings from Yesteryear" in the *Mid-Island Times*.

Professional photographers Nicholas Minervino and Pierre Charbonnet and news cameraman Frank Mallett are also sources. Hicksville natives and longtime residents have generously loaned pictures. Among these donors are the late Helen Hiscock, Mrs. Fred Turner, Robert Berkowitz, Jessie Doyle, Valerie Pakaluk, Minnie Kasten Luhmann, Ruth Schrieber, Medard Ofenloch, Dorothy Brown, Dora Darling, Ben Daines, Joseph Murray, Carl Gellweiler, Joseph Burt, the late Olga Hoebel, Jerry Spiegel, Merle Hawkins Campbell, Joseph Gentile, Joan Wolf, Marite Henessey, Richard Gilison, Ruth Hawkins, Bill McAleer, Bill Muhlenbruck, the Reinhardt family, and the Beniamino family. Personal photographs from the late Gertrude Wetterauer and Runhild Wessell, one-time teaching colleague-friends of the authors, are included, as are lovely ethnic costume pictures from Mr. and Mrs. Sigurd Sjem.

We have drawn on 45 years of readings in the standard Long Island histories, reminiscences, and contemporary accounts of current events. We have received encouragement from all areas of Hicksville life: educators, public library leadership, clergy, business proprietors, club leadership, journalists, students, and countless older residents. Of vital technical assistance has been the unstinting and loving collaboration of Valerie Pakaluk and the gracious patience of her husband Mike Pakaluk.

Local history may not be a panacea for the ills of today's society, but its enthusiasts are as vital to modern man's sanity and progress as are worthy spiritual leaders, teachers, parents, and psychologists.

This logo was adopted for the 350th anniversary of Hicksville's Indian Land Purchase.

INTRODUCTION

Hicksville, the Long Island village with the distinctive and, even to its proud residents, hilarious name, has known and deserved its two-century celebrity. The community is America in microcosm. Here, Sylvania Corporation pioneered atomic fuel elements research on a onetime Algonquian campground, British cavalry foraged from its Colonial roads, and the noble Elias Hicks grazed his cattle. The Long Island Rail Road actually did dead-end its line at the crossroad site for six years. Today, the station is the second busiest on the line.

While much of Long Island was still isolated from the U.S mainland, the community's name was on many lips. Poet Walt Whitman wrote of its early land speculators; German and Irish immigrant ploughmen and gold-beating craftsmen turned the village into a Teutonic spa by the beginning of the 20th century.

Resisting efforts to change its good Quaker name, the growing village was the pickle and potato center of Long Island's agriculture. Its tree-lined streets and crops stretched to the horizons until the golden nematode pest and post-World War II housing developments ushered in the modern era.

In the last 50 years, the population soared from 8,000 to 50,000; every aspect of Oliver Goldsmith's "Sweet Auburn! loveliest village of the plain" was transformed. Schools had to be built and churches and temples expanded; retail and industrial growth was phenomenal. Here, the great plastic industry was pioneered, light industry fed the needs of defense and atomic fuel reactors, and the citizens helped build the LEM module for the astronaut's walk on the moon. Today, Hicksville counts retail ventures in the many hundreds and is the center of bank branch operations and medical insurance operations. A *New York Times* real estate writer recently said, "Hicksville is a place of snug houses and giant stores in mid-Nassau." *Newsday* has said of the village, ". . . it reflects much the best of suburbia."

With good schools, a great and beautiful library, two weekly newspapers, and cultural attractions—such as the Hicksville Gregory Museum, the Long Island Earth Science Center, the state-of-the-art Long Island Reptile Museum and Expo, and a full-scale replica of the Renaissance masterwork *The Gates of Paradise*—Hicksville is visited by thousands of schoolchildren and teachers each year.

Its civic groups are well known. They include the Hicksville Community Council, the Hicksville Historical Society, the Hicksville Youth Council, the Ecumenical Counseling Center, and a vibrant Hicksville Chamber of Commerce. All join with active veteran, fraternal, and service organizations in cooperating to make the community, for all its bustling traffic and commercial downtown, a community whose residential neighborhoods are delightful with flowers, lawns, and garden crops during the long summers.

This book, in its thematic photographs, recalls the story of Hicksville's 350 years. It brings to life a changing yet changeless community, whose name and people bring smiles and recognition worldwide. In Sydney and Perth, Australia, in those Asian places rimming the Indian Ocean, in South and North America, and wherever radio, television, and the printed word communicate, the name Hicksville is known.

Political admirers are even fond of saying at public gatherings: "Hicksville is both the heart and soul of Oyster Bay Town."

Dedicated to our son, Kevin, whose friends were legion.

One

ROOTS

Few Long Island communities can trace their roots back to an Indian land purchase.
—Jesse Merritt, Nassau County Historian, 1948

Hicksville was purchased from the Indians by a Welshman, named for a Quaker, and settled by German immigrants.
—Editor Fred Noeth

The Matinecock Indians once roamed through the Long Island area that includes Hicksville.

Local Native Americans included Matinecocks of the Algonquian stock. Their villages on the North Shore of Long Island were once very numerous, extending from Flushing to Huntington. Fisherman and hunters, as this illustration depicts, they farmed and enjoyed a homeland rich in natural resources. Due to a lack of accessible fresh water in the area of today's Hicksville, the Native Americans preferred to locate their principal villages where rivers and freshwater springs flowed into the sea. The ocean was also their chief food source and provided shells for the manufacture of wampum, an item important to their economy, cultural life, and political relations with warlike mainland tribes. (New York State Museum.)

At the Hicksville Middle School, this Works Progress Administration mural, by Joseph Physioc, depicts Robert Williams's Land Purchase of May 20, 1648. The documentary begins of the histories of Hicksville, Jericho, Plainview, Woodbury, and Syosset. An early settler of Hempstead, the Welshman was a cattle owner and a friend of Matinecock sachem Pugnipan, who wears the artist's fanciful feathered headdress.

Site of the Robert Williams land purchase, the Cantiague Woods is marked by a glacial boulder that in 1745 was placed as a land boundary between the towns of Oyster Bay and Hempstead. Examining this preserved bit of history are, from left to right, the county superintendent of highways; Eugene Nickerson, Nassau's first Democratic executive; and Michael Petito, Oyster Bay town supervisor. Both Nickerson and Petito were part of the 1961 election upset over the long-dominant Republican party.

The spring pond at Jericho was photographed c. 1900. For centuries, Native Americans and Quakers enjoyed the pond's abundance and quality. In this vicinity, with its stands of timber and grazing land, Robert Williams built his home and sought to establish a plantation (settlement). Today's historic Milleridge Inn building was erected to the east of the pond on rising ground. The pond was diverted to the west as the state widened highways and building approached the Long Island Expressway, in the 1960s.

The well-known Milleridge Inn embraces the original home, built in 1672 by Mary Washburn Willets, the sister-in-law of Robert Williams. This historic landmark was spared during the devastation and condemnation wrought by the construction of the Long Island Expressway. The Milleridge proprietor has created a colorful group of shops suggesting a Colonial village, which is one of the Hicksville-Jericho tourist attractions.

Elias Hicks, Jericho's towering Quaker leader (1748–1830) was a self-taught minister who was respected by warring Patriots and Redcoats in the American Revolution. His cattle grazed on what is today's North Broadway. A great voice for antislavery beliefs, his spiritual austerity and teachings created a schism in the Society of Friends. (Local History Room/HPL.)

In Hicksville's early years, Jericho served as the shopping area for the emerging railroad community. The 1788 Quaker Meeting House, built by followers of Elias Hicks, still stands. Here, generations of the Friends have worshiped God, seeking to be animated by "the Inner Light." In the cemetery nearby, Elias and Jemina Hicks rest. (Local History Room/HPL.)

Hicksville has always enjoyed recalling its roots in the Robert Williams Indian Land Purchase. In the memorable 300th Anniversary Commemoration of 1948, Hicksville High School students, in full costume, reenact a Quaker wedding scene during a 90-minute pageant on the school grounds. The actors are Audrey Sutton, witness; Norman Nichols, groom; Jeannine Hicks, bride; Audrey Boos, witness; Homer Bosserman, witness; and Wallace Collins, witness.

Today's Maine Maid Inn in Jericho was the home of Valentine Hicks, Hicksville's namesake. Built in 1789, it is one of the landmarks spared when the Long Island Expressway was built. Valentine Hicks married Elias Hicks's daughter Abigail in 1804. A shipowner and New York City businessman, he moved into this house with his wife and three daughters *c.* 1819. The original building has been enlarged and became the Maine Maid Inn in 1950.

Significant in the Long Island Rail Road's early history was Valentine Hicks, seen in an 1845 portrait by Thomas Hicks. The Jericho leader came out of retirement to join other visionary speculators in chartering the Long Island Rail Road. The Panic of 1837 ruined his plans to direct the railroad through his landholdings toward a New England ferry connection in Greenport. (Nassau County Museum.)

As the second busiest station on the railroad, Hicksville had a colorful early transportation history. Last stop on the railroad after the Panic of 1837 dried up construction funds, Hicksville's first station and roundhouse burned up and two Dewitt Clinton engines, the *Ariel* and the *Postboy*, collided. In this *c.* 1908 westward view, from right to left, are the Herzog store, the junction tracks for the North and South Shore lines, and the second station and freight office. (Heffley Drug Company postcard, Local History Room/HPL.)

Timothy Jackson's Grand Central Hotel, built in 1835, faced the depot for 90 years. The Hicksville prairie site was desolate except for livery stables, and the pie and coffee shops. Streets and house lots laid out by Quaker speculators were empty, except for roaming packs of dogs. A onetime notable guest was New York City's Mayor Gaynor, who recuperated at the hotel with a broken leg, after being snowbound while out hunting during the Blizzard of 1888.

Dominating the Hicksville railroad depot scene for 50 years was the general store of Frederick Herzog and Son. Herzog was typical of German immigrant leaders, such as Frederick Heyne and John Heitz, who bought out the Quaker interests. These enterprising men built up a thriving village during the years 1850 to 1875. Fred Herzog, with his leadership and credit extended to customers, long held Hicksville loyal to the Democratic party. (HGM.)

This religious landmark served as the site of the original Union Chapel in the 1950s, after the Church of Christ mission began its 50-year occupation of the sacred premises. The familiar little church was erected by the Hicksville Methodists in 1900, after the prior building had served young congregations of Lutherans, Reformed Church, and Episcopalians.

In 1850, the Trinity Evangelical Lutheran congregation was organized. This Edward Bady reproduction suggests the pride of Hicksville's oldest congregation as it celebrated 140 years of existence in 1990. The first Lutheran church, located on West Nicholai Street, was erected in 1863. Among the pastors who have served Trinity over its 150 years have been Revs. August Weisel, John Behrens for 44 colorful years, F.G.L. Matchat, O.E.A. Meyer, E.O. Oxee, C.F. Sommer, William Rusch, Edward Stammel, John Krahn, and Wayne Puls.

Hicksville's first Roman Catholics were largely Germans, but it was in this home on Broadway at East Carl Street, the home of the Irish John O'Hara family, that Masses were first celebrated. Standing for almost 140 years until demolished in 1994, the dwelling was visited by missionary priests from St. Monica's Parish in Jamaica and served the congregation since 1854. (HGM.)

Rev. Fr. Theodore Ignatius Goetz laid the cornerstone of the original St. Ignatius Loyola Church on August 1859. The 25-foot by 40-foot structure seated 100 persons and stood on land donated by Henry Pasker. The rectory was erected to the church's north in 1870. This property saw much expansion thanks to the zeal of Fr. Lawrence Fuchs, who served his church and community for more than 50 years. (Local History Room/HPL.)

The little red schoolhouse of Hicksville's early years (1853–1868) was built by family subscriptions. The one-room, clapboard-sided building was located on West Nicholai Street. Heated by a coal stove, it was a place of games at recess, poor attendance, stern discipline, copybooks and readers, a school bell, and the tutoring of younger pupils by their older schoolmates. A favorite pastime of boys was to bait pins with lunch to fish for mice through cracks in the floorboards. (Harold Kelly, Local History Room/HPL.)

Looking every inch the old-time teacher, William Wallace, a Scotsman, was Hicksville's first actual schoolmaster. He replaced James Mathews, who taught in his home. Wallace kept a journal during the 1860s, for which local historians are grateful. He also served as a notary public. (Local History Room/HPL.)

Among the early farming experiments was the growing of sugarcane in today's Broadway Mall area for the production of molasses. The growing of cucumbers for the Heinz Pickling Plant on Bethpage Road was much more successful. (Local History Room/HPL.)

Merritt Horner Sr. was the manager of the Heinz pickle works at the beginning of the 20th century. Seen with Lillian Luehwing Horner, at his leisure, he and his family made their home on Broadway, just south of the Methodist church.

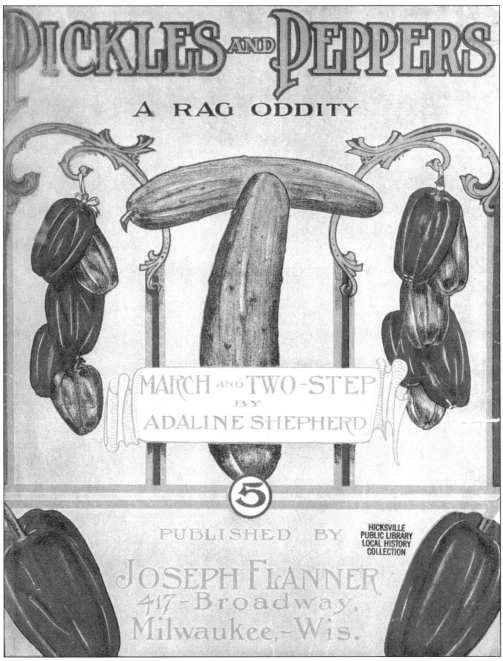

This amusing sheet music was published in 1906, but Hicksville had led the way in Long Island's pickling industry as early as the 1880s. Its three pickle works attracted farmers from all about the village who planted a few acres of cucumbers. H.J. Heinz had a large plant on Bethpage Road until 1922, when a plant disease called the white pickle appeared. It was a profitable agriculture; the cukes underwent various brining processes for sweet, sour, and dill types and were packed in wooden barrels for shipment by rail to Pittsburgh. From the headquarters of the great "57 Varieties," the pickles were bottled and distributed nationally. The pickle-growing and plant operations employed many workers.

Hicksville's gold-beating industry kept New York City markets well supplied with gold leaf, which once decorated many prized objects of ordinary use, including shaving mugs, fine glassware, signs, buggy whips, and buggies. William Munch was in the business and operated several shops. This is his 1908 Richard Street shop. With Munch, second from right, are his workers Clara Navarot, Katy Lecke, Louise Harbach, and Matty Ruth. (HGM.)

A large gold-beating shop in Hicksville was the Mohneberg shop on East Carl Street (today, Goldman Brothers' store parking lot). Mr. and Mrs. Mohneberg stand at left with stalwart gold beaters, who swung 18-pound hammers skillfully for hours, flattening gold pieces into tissue-thin sheets prized by artists and craftsmen. With them are the women and girls who trimmed the gold leaf and deftly placed it into booklets. (HGM.)

Two

'SWEET AUBURN! LOVELIEST VILLAGE OF THE PLAIN'

By 1900, Hicksville was a lovely village with a population of about 1,100 and was part of the new Nassau County. It was a well-known station on the Long Island Rail Road, with dairy farms, pickle plants, gold-beating operations, and retail and artisan facilities for Gold Coast Estates.

The late Nassau County Historian Jesse Merritt recalled Oliver Goldsmith's tribute to England's Auburn at the start of Hicksville's 300th Anniversary in 1948. This 1905 Otto Korten photograph shows a tree-lined, paved Broadway, looking toward the south. (Nassau County Museum.)

Looking north on East Broadway, *c.* 1910, were buildings that are still visible today: St. Ignatius Loyola Church and first parochial school, the sexton's small house on Carl Street, and the Reinhardt Hotel. The post office building on the right was demolished in the 1990s. (Edward Bady, Local History Room/HPL.)

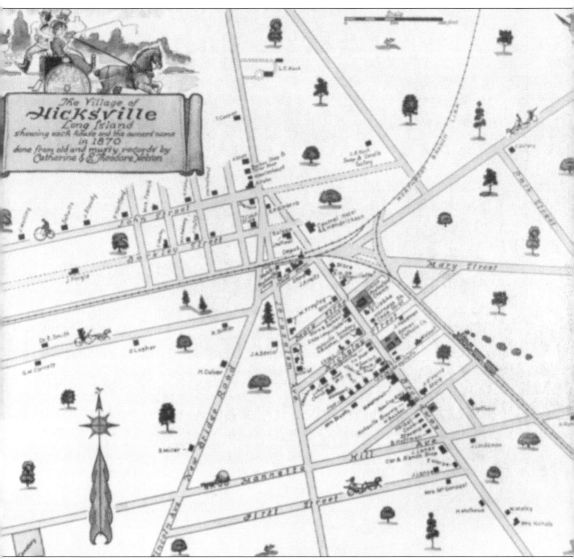

The Catherine and Theodore Nelson pictorial map of Hicksville in 1870 shows 89 buildings and clearly identifies 25 business establishments. The businesses by number and type included seven stores, four blacksmith shops, one stable, one brewery, one hotel, one tinsmith, one soap and candle factory, one private academy, one sash and blind mill, one undertaker, one bowling alley, one saloon, one barbershop, and one harness shop. Built-up streets were Broadway, Jerusalem Avenue, Nicholai Street, West Cherry Street, West Barclay Street, and West John Street. The area east of the railroad was largely undeveloped; the same could be said for areas west of Jerusalem Avenue, south of Duffy Avenue, and north of John Street.

By 1910, Hicksville's railroad scene was one of the busiest. The new station was erected in 1909. Locomotives could be watered from the other side. The train conductor near the touring car and a station flagman control the increasing automotive traffic. The view is to the west at Jerusalem Avenue. (Local History Room/HPL.)

A landmark building, the Old Hicksville Town Hall and Courthouse was erected on land donated by Arnold and Matilda Heitz for the building of the Oyster Bay Town Hall in 1895. The landmark building housed a town justice of the peace and, after 1935, a Nassau Fourth District Court until 1967. The community's needs outgrew the courthouse and the building remained vacant until the Town of Oyster Bay worked out an arrangement with the trustees of the Hicksville Gregory Museum: Long Island's Earth Science Center for the use and preservation of the building. (Local History Room/HPL.)

The most impressive Hicksville political figure until 1919 was Judge Joseph Steinert. His character and his knowledge of the law and public service kept the village a Democratic stronghold for two decades. During his career he served as a justice of the peace; chief justice of the court of special sessions, Queens County; and Oyster Bay town supervisor. (Local History Room/HPL.)

The building at the corner of Broadway and Marie Street has had a colorful history. It housed the Sportsmen's Hotel in the 1880s; a furniture store under Henry C. Huettner, with a face-lift that made it a landmark attraction; the Long Island National Bank; three pharmacies; and today's wicker furniture store. (Local History Room/HPL.)

Hicksville's roots are deep in the lives and the contributions of its pioneer settlers and leaders. Julius Augustin typified the immigrant leaders whose business abilities, love of community, and solid middle-class views built 19th-century Hicksville and similar communities. A Renaissance man, he served as publisher of a German language newspaper and proprietor of general merchandise and a lumberyard. An active member of Trinity Lutheran Church and of the Odd Fellows Organization, he was a highly esteemed Oyster Bay justice of the peace when he died in 1896. (Local History Room, HPL.)

This library was located in the home of Julius and Louise Freytag Augustin, whose daughter Louise Augustin lived here in later years and was the founder of a public library. Redecorated in 1912, this handsome book-filled haven was designed by Louis Comfort of the Tiffany Studio, who created the ceiling and matching stained-glass windows and lampshade. (HGM.)

St. John's Boys Orphanage was a prominent North Broadway site for many years. Located at the current site of the Broadway Mall and Sears Roebuck, St. John's was operated by the Catholic Diocese of Brooklyn and cared for as many as 200 boys. The boys raised most of their own food by crop growing and tending a herd of 50 cows.

By 1908, progressive businesses were adapting to the internal combustion engine steadily. The always innovative Henry F. Huettner department store family delivered furniture and housewares in this stout, right-hand-drive truck. Many customers were North Shore Gold Coast estate magnates. (Local History Room/HPL.)

Horse-drawn delivery wagons were still commonplace well into the 20th century. Here are young examples of free enterprise, the grandchildren of gentleman farmer Henry Puvogel, Henry Jr. and his sister Elsie (mother of the future renowned Hicksville sportsman and journalist Howard Finnegan), ready for some family milk delivery.

Prior to WW I, traveling peddlers often delivered their products in handsome horse-drawn wagons, such as J.H. Bedell's provisions wagon. Families in rural America were usually quite self-sufficient, but it was a great day when deliverymen could bring special meat products to wives "stuck way out in the country." (Local History Room/HPL.)

In the years before WW I, Hicksville was similar to a spa. With a half-dozen hotels, bowling alleys, dance pavilions, baseball diamonds, good solid food, and fresh dairy products, it was a German-American popular vacation place, accessible by railroad. Outside Staehle's Brewery Hotel at the corner of Broadway and West Carl Street, happy couples are dressed for an open-air truck ride. They could either be picnic bound or homeward bound after a great week of fun and games. (HGM.)

Sundays in 1911 brought families and kinfolk together to socialize and take photographs. The Kastens (general store owners) and Schriebers (farmers) were old Dutch Lane neighbors. The Kasten home, seen here, faced north and was demolished in the building of Levitt homes in 1947 and 1948. Families shown are Funfgeld, Wagner, Louring, Bergmann, Meyer, Kehlbeck, Schlick, Keller, Schultz, Theobold, and Ulmer. (Ruth Schrieber, Local History Room/HPL.)

Built in 1914 and photographed in the late 1980s, the first movie house, located on West Nicholai Street, was known to some old-timers as the "uproar house" because of the noise that came from it on Saturday evenings. It sometimes bordered on bedlam with a piano player or playing machine accompanying the silent films and all sorts of disturbances in the balcony, including airborne peanut shells, exploding fireworks, and an occasional pistol shot.

Two men who lost their lives in WW I, Joseph Barry, left, and Charles Wagner, right, are the namesakes of the Joseph Barry Council, Knights of Columbus and the Charles Wagner Post 421, American Legion, respectively. (Local History Room/HPL.)

Weddings and their receptions were unpretentious affairs for the farmers and workers of 75 years ago. Seen in 1918 on the Gellweiler farmstead off Bloomingdale Road are the groom William Murray, the bride Catherine Gellweiler, and the bride's parents Carl (in the Panama hat) and Mary Gellweiler. The maid of honor is Elizabeth Gellweiler. Others in the photograph are unidentified. (Joseph Murray, Local History Room/HPL.)

Joy, festivity, and thanks fills everyone's heart at this grand Armistice supper, held at the St. Stephen's Evangelical Lutheran Church Hall to celebrate the end of WW I. The war ended at the 11th hour on the 11th day of the 11th month in 1918. (Bill Muhlenbruck, Local History Room/HPL.)

Plant nurseries were once common in Hicksville. In 1926, some neighbors pause for a photograph in front of the Kuehen Greenhouses on West Old Country Road. They are Charles R. and Anna Iggulden and sons Bill and Robert, with Mrs. Painter at the left. (Bill Clark.)

Hicksville's population soared from 4,000 in 1920 to 6,772 in 1930. As train commuters multiplied and new housing developments sprang up, more school classrooms had to be provided. The Nicholai Street School, which housed grades kindergarten through 12, had to be supplemented. Built in two stages (1897 and 1909), the now demolished landmark also housed the public library from 1926 to 1950. (HGM.)

Seen on this 1920 graduation day are the following Nicholai Street School students, from left to right: (first row) Joe Healy, Rose Kellner, Anna Sabbatello, Louis Bergold, Minnie Kasten, George Engle, Marjorie Kunz, Doris Brengel, Gertrude Jung, and Kenneth Weickmann; (second row) Helen Augustin, Gertrude Chapman, Mr. Vanderwater, Gladys Rohrbach, Grace Wetterau, and Sidney Hoffman; (third row) George Eisemann, William Schmit, Richard Eisemann, Paul Schaffer, and Edwin Rusch. (HGM.)

The first self-contained Hicksville Junior-Senior High School opened in 1925 on a large tract east of Jerusalem Avenue. The site had once been occupied by a visiting three-ring circus under the big top. This early-1930s view shows the neo-classical school, one of the handsomest in New York State. The WW I cannon trophy was melted down for WW II scrap metal.

As residential growth spread eastward toward Plainview's wide farmland, the East Street Elementary School was erected in 1927, under Principal Nina Plantz. It is still an impressive part of the village's public school system.

Even during the Great Depression, Hicksville had a lot of building under way. Projects included a new Trinity Lutheran Church, the Town Center Building and real movie house, St. Ignatius Church renovations, and the new firehouse shown here. Now enlarged, the firehouse still stands impressively on East Marie Street, the motherhouse for today's three substations. (Local History Room/HPL.)

The village's second firehouse is seen in the 1920s. It was moved across the street on rollers in 1931. Formerly the Firehouse Inn, the building today serves as the popular Peppercorn's Restaurant.

Members of Hicksville High School's senior Honor Society in 1938 are, from right to left, as follows: (front row) Norman Wennagel, Frances McGunnigle, Evelyn Ulmer, Albert Thomas, Margaret Weidner, Sabine Heller, and William Rusch; (back row) Henrietta Braun, Ruth Thiem, Eugene Staehle, Hilda Erb, Kenneth Daugherty (WW II hero bomber pilot), Irene Lampman, Eileen Hux, Harold Huettner, Virginia Karman, and Helen McCabe. (Ruth Thiem Schrieber, Local History Room/HPL.)

For 20 years, starting in 1936, DeMonaco's Fruit and Vegetable Store was a popular downtown Hicksville mecca for food shoppers. Members of the genial proprietor's family appear in their aromatic and colorful market at 111 Broadway, from left to right, as follows: (front row) Jessie DeMonaco (Doyle) and Rosemarie DeMonaco; (back row) worker Eddie Metz, and Mary and Frank DeMonaco.

The contributions of Hicksville to Long Island have often been subtle and significant. In the mid-1930s, well-known and highly-principled surgeon, dentist, and civic leader Dr. Elwood Curtis, left, litigated successfully to keep the formidable N.Y. Parks Commissioner Robert Moses, right, from expanding the Jones Beach development to engulf the Atlantic shoreline beachfront of the Town of Oyster Bay. (Tobay Beach.)

The home of Elwood and Anna Voigt Curtis on West Nicholai Street was a Christmastime showplace for many years. With its chimney-top Santa, reindeer with sleigh, and illuminated front-porch fireplace with stockings, the scene captivated residents and visitors. (Local History Room/HPL.)

This September 1935 wedding dinner for Mr. and Mrs. Charles Lupinek was a happy gathering of family and friends. The glasses raised in toast at Louis Metz's unpretentious Shady Maple

Grove on South Broadway remind us of the unaffected traditional values of America's older immigrant generations, coping with the Great Depression. (Local History Room/HPL.)

When post-WW I home development builders, such as William Levitt, Jerry Spiegel, Anthony Villet, and the Beniamino Brothers, came into Hicksville offering good prices for acreage, farm sales accelerated. The Hicksville Gables development, shown in this aerial view, was located on East Old Country Road. War veterans and their wives bought these roomy Cape Cods for $10,000. The view toward the east (Plainview) is Plainview Road (left), converging with Old Country Road (right). The year is 1949 to 1950, and the farmlands on all sides are in the process of development. In later years, a new Orthodox Jewish Temple was built in the area at the top right, the Redeemer Lutheran Church was erected on the other side of New South Road, and the Long Island Lighting Company was constructed on the farmland at the right. (Bill McAleer, Local History Room/HPL.)

Three

A COMMUNITY
TRANSFORMED

The 1948 Tercentennial Celebration has been called "the Great Divide." For Hicksville, this event brought an end to the days of "Sweet Auburn of the Plain." The fourth 100-year historical phase involved an incredible transformation. Farms disappeared and housing developments, industrial parks, and shopping facilities proliferated. With economic growth came similar transformation in every phase of social life.

As Hicksville neared its 300th anniversary, it was caught up in the great WW II crusade and adventure. Young couples were marrying before the men left for overseas war fronts. The 1942 nuptials of Margaret Duffy and James Stolz united two old and well-known Hicksville families. The bride was the daughter of bank director and farm supply businessman William Duffy; the bridegroom was the son of butcher William Stolz.

James Wilson Joseph Heim Robert Ulmer Henry Gebhardt Patsy Pepe

William Pakaluk Arthur Noeth Raymond Zeltman Melvin Rurbach Wallace Schaefer

Clemes Zglieseky

Henry Wyka

John Zieler

William Remy

Andrew Manelski James Madden John Haughey

More than 20 of Hicksville's sons died during WW II; they rest in far-flung places. Many families of note were represented in this loss.

The great era of Long Island potato crop leadership in the Hicksville-Plainview area began coming to an end in the late 1940s. A parasitical plant pest, the golden nematode, appeared and led to intense U.S. Agricultural Department regulations, which upset local farmers. An old Bulldog Mack truck is loaded with bagged potatoes for trip to Brooklyn Wallabout Market. (Carl Gellweiler, Joseph Murray.)

A name synonymous with "builder, site developer extraordinaire" is Jerry Spiegel. Raised on a Smithtown farm, Spiegel rode the postwar housing building boom to a successful career. Builder of over 1,500 Hicksville homes, he and his Spiegel associates built and owned the memorable Nassau (Hicksville) Farmers Market, extensive commercial property on North Broadway, the 20-acre industrial park on West John Street, and other properties. (Jerry Spiegel, Local History Room/HPL.)

These Bank of Hicksville directors contributed much to the transition, *c.* 1955. They are, from left to right, George H. Hauser, L.L.D.; Dr. Elwood Curtis, D.D.S; Arthur S. Underhill; Elmer H. Kroemer; George C. Karlson, vice president; Henry G. Eisemann, president; Charles C.E. Colthurst, vice president, cashier, and secretary to the board; Ernest R. Jancke; Samuel S. Underhill, executive committee chairman; Morley L. Smith, M.D.; and F.E. Willits, counsel. (Bank Brochure, Local History Room/HPL.)

When commercial banks ruled the banking roost in New York, native son William E. Koutensky and his bank branch managers did much to provide mortgages, loans, and savings facilities for dynamic Hicksville. Among Koutensky's bank "family" were Joseph A. Reinhardt, Gertrude A. Procter, Joseph F. Bayer, Thomas E. O'Brien, Arthur J. Mangan, John Procter Jr., Stephen P. Timoszuk, James Austin, Robert B. Watson, and Joseph E. Dailey. (Local History Room/HPL.)

During the amazing post-WW II growth years, Hicksville's political power resided in the office of Nassau County Clerk Ernest Francke. A veteran Bell Telephone Company lineman, Francke grew up in Hicksville and married Pearl Stoll, the sister of Charles Stoll, a well-known attorney and one-time justice of the peace at the historic Hicksville Courthouse. A local Republican party chairman, Francke ran a very efficient county clerk's office.

Henry G. Eisemann, president of Seaman & Eisemann Insurance, was one of Hicksville's leading benefactors. Never holding elective office, he was still close to political life. He did much to bring the Long Island Lighting Company to Hicksville. Bank director and member of both county and town Planning Commissions, he was a patron of many Hicksville causes. He appears in his office with Leonard Hall, the Republican national leader, and A. Holly Patterson, a Nassau executive. He and wife Florence took delight in his gourmet cooking.

Future Sen. Robert Kennedy campaigns vigorously for his brother Sen. John F. Kennedy at a Nassau Democratic party rally at the Mid-Island Shopping Plaza. The dynamic New Englander carries the political war into the heart of Republican territory.

In October 1959, Pres. Dwight D. Eisenhower is on his way to Oyster Bay for the dedication of the Sagamore Hill home of Theodore Roosevelt as a national historic site. Gov. Thomas E. Dewey accompanies the president, as well-wishers crowd the curbside at the high school. (Local History Room/HPL.)

Opera singer Mimi Benzel helps cut the ribbon at the Mid-Island Shopping Plaza grand opening in 1957. With her, from left to right, are Leonard Frank; Lew Waters, town supervisor; and Walter Stackler. Stackler and Frank, co-owners of the Mid-Island Plaza, had already built many local homes. (Local History Room/HPL.)

One of the first U.S. regional shopping centers was the Mid-Island Shopping Plaza, today's Broadway Mall. A shopping, recreational, and community focal point for 45 years, the retail site greatly changed Hicksville's commercial scene. (Lathrop Douglas, AIA Architect Photograph, Local History Room/HPL.)

Retail growth brought increased traffic, necessitating principal road widening. Railroad elevation trestle supports are in position on Broadway, as Hicksville looks south in 1963. Four blocks of stores on the right side were demolished to widen the avenue.

These baby boomers reflect the large school classes of the Long Island post-WW II population explosion. The St. Ignatius Loyola School Class of 1972 appears at a 1987 reunion. Among those pictured are the following: Marc Atchison, Eileen Bickard-Brown, Terri Lattanzio, Eileen Phelan-Smith, Karen Curley, Rev. Brian McNamara, Andrew Garger, and Roy Harvey; Mary Maier-Huber, Patricia DeFalco, Ann Feeley-Allen, Kevin McCauley, John Lutri, Michael McNamara, Christine Willant, Kathleen O'Connor-Mulligan, Roseann Ferguson-Poggio, Lori Mancini-Lewandowski, Nancy Finn-Calder, Doreen and Lupski Benzie; Dr. John Calamia (former teacher), Regina Krummenacker, Sheila McHugh-Jannace, Toni LaBarca-Roestenberg, Christine Gietschier, Gregory Gambino, Mary Beth Looney-Zurcher, Rita O'Malley-Murphy, Marybeth Coleman, Nancy Johnston-Gallagher, Marianne Crosby, Mary Rogers-McDonald, Alice Sommers-Day, Diane Braja-Hachadoorian, Michael Murphy, Nora Brennan-DiRocco, and Maureen Bungert-Coyle; Douglas Price, Cynthia Van Nostrand, Brian Caglione, Jennifer Eaton-Oldenburg, Daniel Allen, Bernadette McDermott-Costas, Richard Fremglan, Brendan Hilligan, Lawrence Caponegro, Dennis Mezzapesa, Christopher McNamara, Brian Schnurman, Richard Sikorski, Brian Mensching, Thomas Gilbride, Michael O'Connor, and James Monnia. (*Hicksville Illustrated News*, Local History Room/HPL.)

Native son and *Mid-Island Herald* editor and publisher Fred Noeth served Hicksville with a passion and with journalist's skill. He and Joseph Bayer of Long Island National Bank are pictured. Noeth's weekly newspaper traced in its news, features, and editorials the great growth years. He fought heroically but failed in his efforts to incorporate Hicksville. On his death his wife, Sheila Noeth, a journalist of stature, carried on the *Mid-Island Herald* for many years. (Local History Room/HPL.)

As editor and publisher of the *Mid-Island Times*, Robert Morgan, right, served the community with the same courage he showed as a flyer in the U.S. Air Force. He is shown accepting an award from Cmdr. Joseph V. Blazek, left, of the Archie McCord Post, American Legion. Fiercely independent, Morgan could not be compromised by political pressure. He viewed Hicksville's growth pains with realism and lent his newspapers to many worthy causes. His daughter Meg Norris and her husband, Edward Norris, ably succeeded Morgan.

Four
HARMONY IN DIVERSITY

With more than 20 religious congregations and a widening of the ethnic composition of Hicksville, it is a joy to find the public's mature acceptance of the diversity of creed and national origin, which characterizes this community.

These new citizens take the oath of allegiance to the United States during naturalization ceremonies at the Hicksville Middle School in early 1990s. With a long history of harmony in its social diversity, the community's ethnic evolution calmly continues.

In the annals of the Lutheran Church on Long Island, the Reverend P.G.L. Matschat holds a distinguished place. For 43 years (1876–1919), the strong-willed leader of the Trinity Evangelical Lutheran Church provided his people with versatile, dedicated services. A great musical talent, he shared his enjoyment of it. He gave piano, organ, violin, and singing lessons on Saturday mornings; taught German; and played the organ during church services. (HGM, Local History Room/HPL.)

St. Stephens Lutheran Church congregation poses for an anniversary picture in October 1922. This church was established by younger parishioners who wanted an English liturgy rather than the traditional German. (HGM.)

St. Ignatius Loyola Catholic Church before the modernization in 1970 and 1971. Many parishioners recall the rich colors, statuary, and beautiful altar with its mural of St. Ignatius receiving Jesus' inspiration. At the altar for their 1946 wedding are John Hanifan and Rita Rettberg. (Dorothy R. Brown.)

Polish immigrants Maximilian and Valeria Zalewski pose for a portrait. Their daughter, Valerie Pakaluk, longtime assistant editor at Litmor Publications (*Mid-Island Times*), says of her folks: "My parents were more American than many born here, even though they never forgot their homeland. They loved America and what it stood for and encouraged their children (nine) to speak the language and to uphold the laws. Our household was dual language: Polish and English. We struggled with Polish and my parents struggled with English, but we managed and all grew up to be hardworking Americans."

In Hicksville and in San Francisco are located copies of *The Golden Doors*, by Lorenzo Ghiberti, the great Italian Renaissance work of art in Florence. Tradition has it that Michelangelo, stunned by their beauty, christened them the "Gates of Paradise." Consisting of ten large scenes from the Old Testament, the panels are gold leaf on bronze. For almost six centuries, Ghiberti's crowning achievement has been considered important for its exquisite handling of relief, mastery of composition, and as a model for the training of generations of artists. The Gates of Paradise were a gift to Trinity Evangelical Lutheran Church by George C. Karlson, in memory of his wife and son. The doors have brought artistic note to Hicksville since 1971.

By 1960, the Hicksville United Methodist Church was one of Long Island's largest Methodist congregations. At a groundbreaking ceremony are, from left to right, Rev. Henry C. Whyman; Emma Hanson; Rev. Cranston Clayton, pastor; August Deppish; Rebecca Woorell; Ann Carol Melbank; Ray Swarez; Barbara Wicks; John Lice, Boy Scout; Tommy Ehman; and Phillip Robinson, attorney. (Frank Mallett, Local History Room/HPL.)

The groundbreaking ceremony for Hicksville's First Baptist Church was held in March 1958. Since its organization in June 1954, the church had occupied a small building on North Broadway. Officiating at the joyous event were Pastor Richard Grob, right; Leroy Brown, chairman building committee, with the shovel; and George Mardiros, chairman of the board of deacons. The attractive, contemporary building was constructed with volunteer help from members of the congregation. (Local History Room/HPL.)

This photograph by Pierre Charbonnet captures a moment in the village's spiritual life. It shows the altar of St. Ignatius Loyola Roman Catholic Church in the early 1960s, before the beautifully carved interior of the church, built in 1891, was somewhat modernized. The four priests, from left to right, are Rev. Lawrence Ballweg, a youth sports coordinator and the director of a very large religious education program for public school children; Rev. John Vitsas, remembered for his vigorous prayer and homily, hearty camaraderie with parishioners, and staunch patriotism in a controversial war period; Rev. Msgr. George Bittermann, pastor, known as an understanding confessor and counselor and as chaplain of the Joseph Barry Council, Knights of Columbus; Rev. Leo Goggin, assistant pastor, administrator, fund-raiser, and glee club enthusiast. Fathers Bittermann, Goggin, and Vitsas died as pastors; Father Ballweg served as pastor and as director of the Propagation of the Faith before his retirement.

In post-WW II years, the Trinity Lutheran Church flourished and expanded under the leadership of Pastor Edward H. Stammel, who served from from 1942 to 1973. He is shown performing the October 1950 marriage of James Hennessey and Marite Sutter. The groom was an army veteran of WW II, who was also called for service in the Korean War. The bride was the granddaughter of Daniel Sutter, the founder of Sutter Monument Works. (Dorothy R. Brown, Local History Room/HPL.)

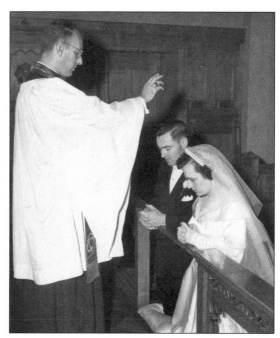

Visible to thousands of Old Country Road motorists is St. Mary's Ukrainian Orthodox Catholic Church. With its onion dome and cross, it evokes thoughts of Orthodox and Byzantine architecture. It was erected in 1938 to satisfy the spiritual needs of the Ukrainian work force who cultivated Hicksville's truck and potato farms. The parishioners had previously worshiped in the Hicksville Methodist Church. First open for services in 1940, the church is still is use and is a reminder of Hicksville's Ukrainian heritage. (HGM.)

Holy Family Roman Catholic Church is one of several parishes formed from mother church St. Ignatius Loyola in the early 1950s. Holy Family has played a vital part in providing for the spiritual needs of three generations of Hicksville's post-WW II Catholics. Its *25th Anniversary Journal* paid tribute to its founding and inspiring pastor, Msgr. Martin O'Dea. Urged to public service by Father O'Dea, the parish's men and women have served on school and public library boards and have performed on stage as members of the Holy Family Players. The church is also known for its exemplary parochial school. (Local History Room/HPL.)

The Orthodox Hebrew Congregation Shaari Zedek (Gates of Righteousness) has made important contributions to Hicksville since its organization in 1919. This synagogue was located on East Barclay Street. Among the founding brotherhood and sisterhood were S. Albert, S. Schwartz, N. and M. Scheiner, K. Hoffman, A. Katz, E. Friedman, S. Kantor, J. Christie, S. Schob, S. Youdelman, and S. Ruhig. Notable leaders also included Rabbi Irving Grossman, Sam Kellner, David Kantor, William Marks, and Morris Rochman.

The Star of David visible in the architecture indicates the second home of the Congregation of Shaari Zedek, which over the years has evolved as a traditional Orthodox congregation with a liberal outlook. The congregation has been served by Rabbis Eli Skaist, Stuart Warner, Jacob Kurland, Melvin Sachs, and young Yosef Korngold. Today, the synagogue is affiliated with the Jewish Heritage Organization, which has attracted many young people.

An ecumenical prayer service is held at St. Ignatius Church in 1975. Joining in prayer and fellowship are, from left to right, Father Costa, pastor of St. Paul's Roman Catholic Church, Jericho; Assistant Pastor Miller, Hicksville United Methodist Church; Father Boyhan, St. Ignatius Church; Reverend MacDonald, pastor at Parkway Community Church; Reverend Perez, pastor at St. Stephen's Evangelical Church; and Reverend Benson, pastor at the United Methodist Church. In the 25 years following this gathering, Hicksville added Greek Orthodox, Indian Pentecostal, Chinese Community, and Hispanic Evangelical churches.

St. Ignatius Catholic Church, rectory, convent, old school, and new school appear in this 1954 aerial photograph. The property embraces an entire block on Broadway between East Nicholai and Cherry Streets. Acquisitions and remodeling by Pastor Reverend Fuchs, Pastor Hauck, and Rt. Rev. George Bittermann resulted in a new rectory, a parochial school, and a convent for the teaching sisters.

Polish National Alliance youth are seen entertaining in traditional costumes at the Hicksville Gregory Museum. The program was part of a three-day commemoration of the community's 325th anniversary. The young people were recalling the Polish ethnic contribution in Hicksville's great farm era.

During the Robert Williams 325th Anniversary fete, the Hebraic contributions were recalled spiritedly by these Hicksville High School students, singing Israeli folk songs. The historical pageants won a Freedom's Foundation Award for Hicksville.

Rev. Canon Domenic Ciannella, affectionately known as Father "Dom," served Holy Trinity Episcopal Church for 34 years. He is shown greeting Roman Catholic friends Carolyn and Bill Kelly and Anthony Previte after the cleric's retirement Mass of Thanksgiving. He is remembered for his sonorous and splendid presence at liturgies and as an excellent homilist and a courageous expansionist. His was a socially oriented pastorate from the beginning. Cofounder and host for the Hicksville Interfaith Nutrition Network—which has fed Hicksville's homeless, impoverished, and senior citizens of small means—he was proud of Hicksville's history and was a founding member of the Hicksville Historical Society. His was an ecumenical view and his non-Episcopalian friends were legion. (Richard Evers, Local History Room/HPL.)

To enter Holy Trinity Greek Orthodox Church is to find oneself in the world of Byzantine iconography. On all sides in this church on Field Avenue—Hicksville's "Gold Coast"—are paintings of Jesus, the Virgin Mary, angels, and saints in vivid colors. (Local History Room/HPL.)

An awesome ceiling icon of Christ was created by renowned iconographer George Filipakic, a member of the Greek-American congregation, which offers an impressive Greek language program for children. (Local History Room/HPL.)

Officers of Hicksville's Ancient Order of Hibernians and ladies' auxiliary receive an American Flag that flew over the nation's Capitol. Pictured from left to right in this 1977 presentation are Jim Cummings, public relations specialist, correspondent for the *Irish Echo*, and columnist for the *Hicksville Mid-Island Herald*; U.S. Rep. Norman Lent; Jean Clark; Patrick Cowan; and John Campbell.

Olga Sjem, born in 1915 in the United States, appears in Ukrainian folk costume. Her parents took her to the Ukraine during WW I and came back to the United States when she was 5 years old. She married Sigurd Sjem, a butcher and delicatessen owner, and had a son and a daughter, William and Lara, graduates of Hicksville public schools. (Olga Sjem, Local History Room/HPL.)

Hicksville's third church group, the Reformed Church, has evolved over the last 50 years into the remarkable force for community good known as the Parkway Community Church. Here, liturgy, faith, and good works combine to assist many disoriented people who are alcoholics, drug afflicted, homeless, or adrift. When the Joseph Barry Council, Knights of Columbus, honored Rev. Douglas MacDonald with its community service award, it honored a pastor esteemed by people of many faiths. MacDonald appears at the far left with part of a 1955 confirmation class.

At a family wedding, Fr. Marion Justin Reinhardt poses with his grandniece Joan Lauck, right, and another flower girl. He eventually became a monsignor and served for many years as the presiding magistrate of the Marriage Tribunal of the Roman Catholic Diocese of Brooklyn. A descendent of the Lauck-Reinhardt clans, he was a graduate of St. Ignatius Church School, a civil law instructor, a canon lawyer, and a great influence on efforts to facilitate marriage annulment proceedings in the United States. Through his patient and scholarly efforts, the Vatican and greater Catholic world came to appreciate numerous sociological and psychological grounds for invalidity in a marriage ceremony. He was fond of saying, "I've had my ecclesiastical home in various places, but my real residence was in Hicksville." In the 1990s, the affable gentleman often took lunch in Hicksville. He enjoyed visiting the Hicksville Public Library Local History Room and talking about his Hicksville roots.

Five

THE WORLD OF
SPORTS AND CLUBS

"America is a nation of joiners." Athletic team and community club membership has long enriched Hicksville's life. Our understanding of democracy stems from our work on committees, volunteerism, and team sportsmanship, which are large parts of the American creed. Hicksville is no exception.

In the bicycle craze of the 1890s, these enthusiasts pose before a ride through Hicksville and Jericho. Second from right is Helen Bacon. She later married Julius Augustin and became the mother of Helen Augustin, who married Mr. Hiscock, lived in Garden City Park, and was a foremost benefactress of the Hicksville Gregory Museum. (Edward Bady, HGM.)

Standing proudly with hometown admirers is Hicksville's Jerome Steinert, a member of the U.S. bicycle team, which took third place in the 1912 Olympic Games 200-mile race. Steinert was the nephew of Judge Joseph Steinert, longtime Democratic leader. (HGM.)

H.F. Grant, in his victorious ALCO car, passes through Hicksville in the 1910 Vanderbilt Cup Race. The first race in 1904 brought out huge crowds, resulting in injuries and a death that caused Vanderbilt to build his own motor parkway. (Nassau County Historical Museum.)

Talk about traffic jams . . . this is Broadway in Hicksville c. 1910, when car-owning sports were fender to fender in an effort to get anywhere. Was it to get vantage spots from which to view the Vanderbilt Cup Races? (Nassau County Historical Museum.)

For 20 years, Northeast dirt tracks roared to the racing of Mike Caruso's midget cars. Ex-Marine Mike Nazaruk and one-legged Bill Schindler drove Caruso's little cars with their oversized pistons to many victories. Caruso's success came from his mechanical ability to cut down engines salvaged at his junkyard and from old limousines towed from Long Island's Gold Coast estates. Mike won Midget Racing Car Hall of Fame membership in 1981. (Local History Room/HPL.)

The uniformed boys of the Hicksville Junior Fire Department reflect the recent 1898 American war with Spain. Impatient to join the adult firefighters are, from left to right in the middle row, Andrew Heberer, Julius Heberer with Philip Ofenloch holding the leather water bucket, and Joseph Ofenloch. Many families have had generations of volunteer firefighters. (Local History Room/HPL.)

This night fire occurred on West Broadway in downtown Hicksville in the 1960s. Toxic fumes and smoke make even a seemingly small fire dangerous for volunteer firefighters. Damaged interior floors can collapse under the weight of firemen intent on locating residents overcome by smoke. (Frank Mallett.)

The Plainview Gun Club held a meeting at Muhlenbruck's Saloon (today's North Shore University Hospital) in 1912. Pictured from left to right are the following: (front row) Mr. Fleischer; Henry Puvogel, later a Hicksville realtor; unidentified; and Louis Hoebel, a Hicksville farmer; (middle row) unidentified; John Jantzen, a farmer and director of Long Island National Bank of Hicksville; Richard Muhlenbruck; and Mr. Menger, a former New York City politician and a Plainview School Board trustee; (back row) unidentified; John Rugen; unidentified; Peter Peter; unidentified; and Henry Muhlenbruck, proprietor and club founder. (Olga Hoebel, Local History Room/HPL.)

Giants did not dominate the basketball courts of yesteryear. Here are the members of the Hicksville High School basketball team, *c*. 1924. Tom Morselli was the tallest player. Others were Harold Bergold; Clarence Heller; Walter Schlicting, team captain; Tom Kearny; Eddie Donati; and Lou Millevolte, the future school athletic director.

In the early decades of the 20th century, baseball was played on Hicksville's many baseball diamonds. The Crescents of Hicksville included, from left to right, the following: (front row) Al Rave, Tom Lang, Dave Steinert, August Fassender, William McKenna, and mascot Eddie Rave; (back row) manager J. Puvogel, Ed Schriber, William Kerbs, August Schnepf, umpire Al Hersfield, assistant manager Jerome Steinert, Charles Schmidt, secretary Fred Peters, Frank Fuessel, and scorer Joseph Steinert. (Bill Clark.)

At the 1931 New York State Firefighters Tournament at Troy, Hicksville's Hicks racing team took the state championship. Under Capt. John Jeanson, the Hicks captured eight first-place trophies and set five new state records. The champions were Chief John Puvogel, John Jeanson, Joseph Braun, Gerard Braun, John Werthessen Jr., William Braun, Otto Jeansen, Harold Hawxhurst, Richard Kershaw, John Werthessen, former Chief Louis Fricke, Arnold Jeansen, John Miller, William Geyer, Vincent Stolz, Harry Borley, Edmund Needer, Valentine Kerbs, and William Cisler. By the millennium Year 2000, the Hicksville's Fire Department was well known for having hosted 75 annual parades and firefighters' tournaments and drills. Held on Labor Day, the great parade and thrilling firefighters' drill competition draws thousands of volunteer firefighters and their families from all over the state. (Edward Bady, Local History Room/HPL.)

Today's Hicksville American Baseball League is a lively echo of these 1934 high school diamond champions. Pictured from left to right are the following: (front row) J. Leonard, C. Sauer, W. Muench, K. Maas, and M. Rennie; (middle row) E. Hoagland, H. Schaaf, A. Kishanuk, W. Pakaluk, and E. Emmel; (back row) Coach Harold Bergold, W. York, ? Benecke, M. Darmorhay, H. Guckenberger, Pete Sitnik, Ray Stock, Frank Pubins, and Bill Payoski. (Local History Room/HPL.)

Service clubs encourage fellowship and good works among professionals and businessmen. The 1939 Kiwanis Club enjoys lunch at the Hicksville Inn on Broadway. Pictured from left to right are the following: (front row) Dr. Milhauser; Leon Galloway, teacher; Morris Rochman, attorney; Tony Mussel; Dr. George Laucks, chiropractor; Dr. Charles Masek, dentist; Bill DeFensis, printer; John Staryk, dairyman; Bill Kemp, Gulf service station; and Dr. Bob Ferdinand, dentist; (back row) unidentified; Jay Smith, druggist; Dr. Walter Stillger; unidentified clergyman; Frank Chlumsky, town councilman; Percy Maud, printer; unidentified; and Archie Mohen, funeral director.

"Uncle" Frank Chlumsky, second from left, exemplified the American joiner, club person, and public servant. With him are Judge Julius Schwartz and Democratic party leader Fred Sutter, right. Chlumsky's 65 years of joyful and astute leadership in Hicksville has never been equaled. Self-educated and a cigar maker by trade, he came to this village as a young man. Founder of the Hicksville Chamber of Commerce, he served as member and president of the Board of Education from 1919 to 1943, when he began his 12-year role as a Town of Oyster Bay councilman. He was a leader of the Kiwanis Club, director of the Salvation Army for many years, treasurer of the fire department, and director of the Servicemen's Comfort Committee during both World Wars. In his 90s, he served as the installing officer of the Hicksville Community Council. He lived to the age of 97.

Between 1928 and 1947, the Long Island Aviation Country Club made flying history just south of Hicksville. Here, clubhouse, pool, tennis courts, and plane hangars are visible. Charles A. Lindbergh taught his wife, Anne Morrow Lindbergh, to fly from this field, where notable aviators and the Gatsby set housed their aircraft. (*Life* magazine, Bill Clark.)

Lions Club Awards Night in 1956 honored youngsters for good citizenship and scholarship. Trophies were presented to Kathy Kapsol, East Street School; Leon Kanawanda, Hicksville Junior High School, future Vietnam War army captain, and doctor; Barbara Middleton, Trinity Lutheran School; Linda Kulbaba, Burns Avenue School; Steven Bourn, Nicholai Street School; Jerome Waters, St. Ignatius Loyola School; and Albert Fromm, Woodland Avenue School. (Frank Mallett, Local History Room/HPL.)

The 1936 Hicksville High School Football Team, known as the North Shore Champs, is seen, from right to left, as follows: (front row) Dick Rennie; Fred Fluckinger; Harry Schluter; Harold Mayer, captain; Philip Pignatara; Merrill Yarotzkey; Peter Damorhay; and John Protina; (middle row) James LaFlare; George Hannigan; Arthur McInnes; Joseph Leonard; John Jablonsky; Eugene Staehle; Samuel Englebretson; Charles Saurer; George Carnes; and John Zulkofske; (back row) Michael Presloch, "coach"; Ed Yutzler; Vincent Lauck; Peter Rohback; George Livingston, manager; Norman Lovitt; Warren Graef; unidentified; Myron Wawryck, assistant manager; Henry Hawkins; Harry Jung; Russell Cornwall; and Louis Millevolte, assistant coach. The cheerleaders, from right to left, are as follows: Stanley Mczrokowski, Virginia Karman, Gloria Garbarino, Stephanie Browdowchik, Helen McCabe, Lucille Ruggiero, and Abie Albert.

The Hicksville Community Council, founded in 1970, has served for 30 years to bond community organizations. A forum and nonvoting body, the council has avoided politics and divisive partisanship. Sheila Noeth, the founder of the council and the editor of the *Mid-Island Herald*, stands at the right during this Hicksville Public Library meeting. Among those on the left are Olga Hoebel, local artist; Gardiner Gregory, museum founder; Ann Gregory, recording secretary; Walter Gebhardt, Carpenters' Union shop steward; Fire Marshal John Specht; Denward Collins Jr.; Kenneth Barnes; Frank Chlumsky; and Rev. Domenic Ciannella. Among those on the right are Neil McCormack, Tom Nagle, Rosemary Barrow, and Caleb Hornbostle. (HGM, Local History Room/HPL.)

In his big game hunter's lair, Judge Charles Stoll, center, shows a walrus tusk trophy to community leaders Dr. Walter Stillger Jr., Charles Bartels, and his law partner Aaron Rochman. Stoll, a former Oyster Bay town justice of the peace, hunted while on vacation. The Stoll large animal exhibit at the Vanderbilt Museum in Centerport is the repository for some his fine trophies. (HGM, Local History Room/HPL.)

Every national holiday, "Old Glory" flies on Hicksville's downtown streets. War veterans of Charles Wagner Post 421, American Legion, pause while posting the national colors on July 4, 1998. Pictured from left to right are Andy Malone; Herbert Grimmer; Kurt Surhoff; Henry Arias; Raymond Gamble, veteran of D-Day, Iwo Jima and Okinawa landings; Fred Hoehing; Neil McInnis; Frank Rybak; Robert Kluck; and Cmdr. John Mauro. The little patriot is Zachary, grandson of Fred Hoehing. (Dick Evers, Local History Room/HPL.)

During the great era of volunteerism, 1965 to 1975, this reunion of the Gregory Museum "family" of volunteers and workers—who have made the Long Island Earth Science Center a wondrous place—was held. Volunteers, from left to right, are as follows: (front row) Rosemary Barrow; Anne Evers; Gussie Daines; Val Conover; Elizabeth Pierce; Diana Kean; Isobel Koressler; and Kathleen Young; (middle row) Marilyn and Dick Schuler; Gardiner and Ann Gregory, museum founders; Amy Curran; Frances Bianculli; John Kean, president; Grace Bady; Julie Clark; Sr. Pat O'Connell; Ben Daines; Joseph Vajdak, director; Donald Curran; John and Joyce Shaw; Richard Evers, past president; Warren Barrow; and Ken Henrie. (Edward Bady, HGM.)

The Hicksville Junior High School National Junior Honor Society dressed up for this April 1961 photograph. Principal and school alumnus Bernard Braun proudly leads the "largest junior high school under one roof, in the state of New York," in the early years of Hicksville's innovative three-track system. They all look like youths who have noble goals. (HGM, Local History Room/HPL.)

The frequency of Boy Scout Eagle Courts of Honor tells us much about a community. New Eagle Scout Fred Harvey stands proudly with Oyster Bay Town Supervisor John Venditto and Kevin Kremler, assistant scoutmaster, right. Sharing this proud moment are his parents, Mr. and Mrs. Bill Harvey, and his brother William Harvey. Both brothers went on to attend the U.S. Naval Academy. (Local History Room/HPL.)

Older sports fans still recall the great semiprofessional football seasons when the Hicksville Field Club vied successfully for many gridiron championships. Here are the 1951 Nassau County Semipro Champions (12 Wins, 1 Loss), from left to right: (front row) (9) unidentified; (34) Walter Biesse; (36) Leo Ruggiero; (22) Bob Quinlin; (8) Bill (Gabby) Garbarino (deceased); (21) unidentified; (30) Tippy Messina; and (13) unidentified; (middle row) (4) George Karman; (5) Jerry Calandrillo; (20) unidentified; (23) Pat Hennerty; (6) unidentified; Ralph Straub; (7) Mike Greggo; and (14) Stan Knudsen; (back row) Dom Sabatella, coach; (33) George Histon; (10) George Thomas; (3) George (Big Wink) VanWickler; (24) Fred Fluckinger; (2) Joe (Smith) Switala; (35) unidentified; Ed Coleman; (32) unidentified; (17) Ray Halleran (deceased); (15) Sid Rigby; (1) Tom Hennerty; (19) "Mike" Way; Bill York (in suit); and (29) Myron Dahmorahy.

Although salaried, political leaders spend much of their time in quasi-volunteer activities. Honored by the Hicksville Chamber of Commerce at its annual dinner-dance are, third from left, Richard Evers, local historian; and, holding citations, Anne Evers, "Citizen of the Year," and Don LeCompte, "Small Businessman of the Year." With them in the center is Town Councilman Tom Clark. Others are Councilwoman Christine J. Preston, Councilman Len B. Symons, Nassau County legislator Edward Mangano, Nassau Comptroller Fred Parola, New York State Assemblyman Marc Herbst, Town Supervisor John Venditto, Chamber of Commerce President Patricia Conway, County Executive Tom Gulotta, scholarship winner Payal Suchdev, and Town Clerk Fannie L. Corsentino.

At this millennium luncheon, the Hicksville Chamber of Commerce honors those who have served as chamber president over the years: Beth Dalton Costello, Marc Ramirez, Patricia Conway, Effie Krogmann, Oyster Bay Town Supervisor John Venditto, Ella Marie Columbo, Henry Brengel, and Constance Clarke. Together, they have become generation of community leaders

Six

FEMININE MYSTIQUE

The roles and contributions to society of women are increasingly the focal point of historians, political scientists, and economists. In Hicksville over the last century, one can trace much of the mystique, the natural capacity, infusing women. While homemakers, wives, and mothers, Hicksville women have expressed and fulfilled themselves in myriad ways.

Sr. Catherine "Kitty" Heilig, a graduate of Hicksville's public schools (Class of 1940) entered the Maryknoll Order for a missionary's calling. For over 40 years, she engaged in arduous, often dangerous, work with the people of largely undeveloped areas of South America. She served farmers living in very small and isolated Bolivian communities along the rivers. She assisted people who are unaware of each other and unknowing of the resources and skills that could improve their lives: literacy, nutrition, and health care. She faced hardships and diseases rampant within the wet jungles. Known by her Spanish name "Catica," the sister's name once appeared on a list of "agitators," those who taught and raised the level of consciousness among the poor. This noble lady says of her work, "God's reign of justice will come when we can share and learn with and from one another. The injustices will delay the coming but we are on the road which leads that way."

The community once had numerous dress factories, and the first one was that of William Wetterauer on East John Street. In 1912, these full and part-time workers of the Hicksville Dress Company dressed up for a company picture. They are, from left to right, as follows: (first row) unidentified, Louise Wetterauer, Nancy Kramer (Eisemann), Helen Betcha, unidentified, Marie Vetter, and unidentified; (second row) Louise Lenzer, unidentified, unidentified, Lydia Frey (Salzgaber), unidentified, Katie Hoberg, unidentified, and unidentified; (third row) Katie Klug, unidentified, unidentified, Mrs. William Wetterauer, and several unidentified; (fourth row) William Wetterauer, William Betcha, unidentified, and Margaret Vetter. (HGM, Local History Room/HPL.)

Company picnics and boss-sponsored beach parties at Bayville gave the Wetterauer Dress Factory girls a day to don their woolen bathing suits and caps. The enviable male worker had the local belles all to himself. Pictured, from right to left, are unidentified, Hilda, Louisa L., Josephine G., and Nona G. (Gertrude Wetterauer, Local History Room/HPL.)

Susan Metakis and her daughter, Nicole, represent the basic aspect of the mystique which is womankind: the perpetuation and nurturing of the human species. In 1987, the mother exposes her child to the presence and the appearance of animals at the Malcomb farm, long a part of the Jericho Historic Preserve. (Richard Evers.)

Can we squeeze in one more? Plainview and Hicksville stylish ladies take a ride in the WW I era. The two ladies at back right are sisters Anna and Elizabeth Schrieber. (Ruth Schrieber, Local History Room/HPL.)

Hicksville High School opened in 1925. It had a single gymnasium and served both genders. These basketball players wear the legendary physical education bloomers and blouse that characterized girls' gym classes. Gertrude Wetterauer, second from the right, went on to be a world-traveling, high school social studies chairman in the 1960s. (Local History Room/HPL.)

During the first decade of the 20th century, the age of the automobile arrived. Facing east at the corner of Carl Street are Frank and Catherine (Kramer) Piquet, bundled up in this eye-catching roadster, ready for a ride along Broadway. Mary (Koehler) Martens of Woodbury Road, the Piquets' next-door neighbor, said of the driver pictured in this *Mid-Island Herald* photograph, "he was a devil about cars and was one of the first people I knew to own one." Dr. William G. Burke, a well-known surgeon, later had his office on the lot visible behind the rear of the roadster. (HGM, Local History Room/HPL.)

At this party held *c.* 1912, children dance around a Maypole and celebrate the birthday of Helen Augustin Hiscock, who in her later years earned a Skidmore College degree and, with her husband, was active in the Episcopal church. For 30 years, she was a devoted benefactor of the Historical Committee of the Hicksville Gregory Museum. Her grandparents Mr. and Mrs. Julius Augustin were lumberyard owners and community leaders. The birthday party took place right where today's parking field for the Delco Plaza Shopping Center stands. (HGM, Local History Room/HPL.)

Teaching has long been considered a traditional and suitable form of women's work. To this vital vocation, generations of women have brought learning, spirit, manners, and imagination. These mentors of our grandparents' day sit poised and proper with Principal Vanderwater.

The legacy of educators is their influence on the lives of the students they have touched. So it is with Mabel R. Farley, who, for nearly 50 years, motivated and enriched the lives of Hicksville students. To a legion of graduates, she represented what education was all about. She came to Hicksville in 1912 from a state teacher's college. She was principal of Hicksville High School for 31 years and on retirement was a member of the School Board. This exemplary lady was admired and beloved by three generations of Hicksvillites.

A 1919 Hicksville High School girls' field hockey team played against foes such as Amityville, Westbury, and Mineola. The team was a formidable adversary. Members, from left to right, are as follows: (front row) Georgianne Stiehler, Dinah Anderson, Mary MacIntosh, Evelyn Staehle, Jeanette Loeffler, and Gertrude Korfitzen; (back row) Coach Horobin, Doreathea Miller, Katherine Stiehler, Theresa (Pete) Kiesel, Helen Klingelhoeffer, Alice Margot, and Viola Kuhne. (Howard Finnegan, *Hicksville Illustrated News*, Local History Room/HPL.)

Before WW II, eastern Nassau County was still very rural, with farms and a North Shore glacial moraine covered with forests. Rod-and-gun clubs were common; bridle paths crisscrossed the island, luring riders to startling vistas and moments of remote solitude. These stylish high school equestrians project an image of Hicksville femininity, filling a modern heart with longing for the faces and times gone by. (Local History Room/HPL.)

In pageant costumes in 1948, these high school teachers are ready to parade in Hicksville's 300th Anniversary Celebration. Runhild Wessell taught German and, in retirement years, went into the county jail to tutor inmates on a person-to-person basis. Gertrude Wetterauer, center, social studies teacher, chaired the Tercentennial Commemoration. Ruth Daley is remembered for her sense of humor as she dispensed health course wisdom. (Local History Room/HPL.)

Olga Hoebel, Hicksville's resident artist, holds her pet fox and sits on the prairie that was part of her husband's Hicksville farm. This talented woman founded the Independent Art Society of Long Island and was known for her Adirondack nature works and portraits. Her miniatures are prized treasures. Born in Moscow, her pharmacist-father was employed under the czar. Her early art training was by Van De Vorde in the Kaiser's wartime Germany.

Hicksville's Deborah "Arnie" Arnesen may not have been included among the moral giants in John F. Kennedy's *Profiles in Courage*, but the four-term state representative from Orford, New Hampshire, vied for the post of governor of New Hampshire in 1992—a Democrat in the teeth of a largely Republican electorate. Her lost cause notwithstanding, the High School Hall of Famer is counted among emerging state leaders nationwide. She has been New Hampshire's director of the Civil Liberties Union. A member of the Commerce, Small Business, and Consumer Affairs Committee in the House, she counts environment concerns, educational aid, property tax relief, reform, and accessibility of health insurance as her causes.

"The whole world loves a bride." "Every girl on her wedding day is beautiful." Certainly, the thoughtful observer stands in awe of the radiance that suffuses a bride. Here post-WW II baby boomer Paulette Beniamino enjoys her wedding day. She poses with her dad, Bernard "Jim" Beniamino, a contractor who helped build the Hicksville Gables housing development. Paulette went on to become a licensed practical nurse specializing in nursing home supervisory work. (Beniamino family, Local History Room/HPL.)

"Airline stewardesses should be attractive, well groomed, courteous—from 21 to 28 years of age, 5 feet 5 to 5 feet 6 inches tall and not over 130 pounds." Hicksville Junior High ninth-graders are spellbound by a real stewardess during Career Week in 1960. (HGM, Local History Room/HPL.)

An exultant Ann Gregory enjoys her retirement party, after 16 years of impressive contributions to the Hicksville Gregory Museum, which was founded by her husband, Gardiner Gregory, who appears to be equally happy. Her leadership in recruiting and motivating more than 260 volunteers and local business contributors was a veritable tour de force. Sharing the joy is Dorothy H. McGee, left, Oyster Bay Town Bicentennial commissioner—herself an exemplary woman. (HGM, Local History Room/HPL.)

The opening of the doors of the U.S. Military Academies to women to brought Nancy Harman to the 1977 plebe class at West Point. Ranking eighth in her Hicksville High graduating class, the captain of the swimming team, and sister of a decorated reconnaissance helicopter pilot with two tours in Vietnam, she was among the pioneering young women opting for military academies. Her life has been a true reflection of the mystique, which is women: marriage to a fellow cadet, Army Intelligence service, motherhood, and reservist service in the Gulf War. (Edward Bady, Local History Room/HPL.)

Grace J. Fippinger of Hicksville High's Class of 1944 was an outstanding corporate leader for 20 years. She was the first woman executive of the Bell System. She was vice president, secretary-treasurer of NYNEX Corporation at her retirement in 1990. A graduate of St. Lawrence University, she was a member of numerous community and business boards. Among her honors was the John Peter Zenger Award for outstanding service and achievement from the Nassau County Press Association. She was appointed by Gov. Nelson Rockefeller to the New York State Women's Council and, at Gov. Hugh Carey's request, served on the Economic Development Advisory Council. A devout Catholic, she was proud of her farming family and recognized as her inspiration her aunt Emily Fippinger, a founder of the Hicksville Public Library, a teacher, and a world traveler.

Seven

A SONG IN OUR HEART

Music has often enriched Hicksville's cultural and ceremonial life. Whether we just listen or make music, the beat and the melodies make our hearts sing and animate our public and private lives.

Among the Hicksville light industries with a low-key operation—often unknown to the majority of the residents for much of its 25 years in the village—was the Hohner Company Inc., manufacturers of the world-famous harmonica line. The above old-time advertisement recalls a less technical age, when boys and girls made their own entertainment with a pocket harmonica and a self-teaching Hohner instruction booklet.

A brass band of pre-WW I provides parade music. Pictured from left to right are the following: (front row) Mr. Gebhardt, Arthur Huettner, and unidentified; (back row) Henry Puvogel, George Forgie, Frank Jung, Fred Turner, Frank M., and unidentified. (Mrs. Fred Turner, Local History Room/HPL.)

The winner of the World Open Drum and Bugle Corps Championship—eight out of nine competitions—the St. Ignatius Girls Cadet Corps thrilled audiences all over the United States and Canada with its splendid music and disciplined panoply. Shown is the Cadet Corps' color guard and banner, with Rev. Fr. Fred Harrer, participating in a 1970 Flag Day parade. This was a distinctive era in community music, a time when older teenage girls were open to the inculcation of self-discipline and espirit de corps.

This photograph reminds us of the German-American fondness for hearty male choral groups. The Saengerrunde was a singing society whose meeting and rehearsal place was Staehle's Brewery Hotel at West Broadway and Carl Street. Active from 1900 to 1910, members included mature men, prominent in the village's trades and businesses. Seen here, from left to right, are the following: (front row) Bill Weickmann, gold beater; Ludwig Birseck, director of the group; Eugene Staehle, Brewery Hotel proprietor; and possibly Mr. Reidlinger; (second row) A. Kaule, worker in Sutter Monument Works; unidentified; Mr. Albrecht, ice-cream store owner; and Bill Stolz, butcher; (third row) unidentified; William Matschat, whose father was Trinity Lutheran pastor; John Banschbach, postmaster; and Richard Sutter, uncle of Fred Sutter. The gentleman at the left rear is unknown, although he was first thought to be Pres. Theodore Roosevelt, whom the Saengerrunde entertained at Sagamore Hill. (HGM, Local History Room/HPL.)

Billy Joel grew up in a Levitt housing development in Hicksville; so, he is fond of recalling Levitt facilities such as swimming pools, Village Greens, the schools, church dances, and the old downtown of Hicksville. Here, Joel and his first combo, the Lost Souls, are at the New York Pavilion of the New York Worlds Fair, 1965. They are competing in a battle of the bands, in which they were barely bested by a trio from Hewlett. Contest promoter John McGuin is at the left with Billy Joel; the late, great Howie Blauvelt; Jim Bosse; Ken Recher; and Rosemary Walsh, codirector of the Hicksville Public Schools Recreation Department. (Photographed copy by Edward Bady of *Mid-Island Herald* picture by press photographer Drennen, Aug. 12, 1965. HGM, Local History Room/HPL.)

As Hicksville developed a rich musical school, expression kept pace with the village's growth during the period 1955 to 1975. Here is the junior high school music department in the 1960s: skilled, versatile and enthusiastic. From left to right, they are Henry Gates, Vincent Detrinis, Robert Pownall, Peter Borst, Donald Sitterly, Robert West, Richard Been, Miss Litwak, and Joseph Tuminello. (Local History Room/HPL.)

All ready for a junior high Fine Arts Week concert are these handsome members of a mixed eighth- and ninth-grade choir, with music department chairman Henry Gates at the right. The large group reflects those incredible years when the junior and senior high schools were graduating more than 1,000 students a year. (Local History Room/HPL.)

An early classical influence on Billy Joel was longtime Hicksville resident Morton Estrin, the internationally known pianist. Estrin is proud of Joel's "very special gifts." The pianist is acclaimed for his mastery of difficult works by Chopin and Beethoven. A superb interpreter of romantic music, often of neglected masterpieces, he is a senior member of the Hofstra University music faculty. He has performed at the Hicksville Public Library. (Robert Berkowitz, Local History Room/HPL.)

During the American Revolution bicentennial years, many Hicksville youngsters and the then available adult leadership belonged to the Boys and Girls Scouts, the Campfire Girls, the 4-H Club, and the Police Boys Club. At the grand opening of the elevated station of the Long Island Rail Road in 1964, were the always sharp, well-drilled Nautical Cadets Band of the Nassau County Police Boys Club.

Rosemarie, by Rudolf Friml, lit up the stage in 1945. It was typical of the lavish musical productions undertaken over 50 years by the students and musical faculty of the public schools.

Charles Gouse, the supervisor of music, directs the Hicksville Community Orchestra, which was sponsored by the Recreation Department of the Hicksville Public Schools during the 1960s and 1970s. The musicians ranged from youths to senior citizens, practiced weekly, and performed for audiences on a regular basis.

"A singing community is a happy community" was the motto of the Hicksville Choral Society for over 35 years. During that time, 1923–1948, the musical group contributed greatly to make this motto a truth. They believed that music is a universal language and that the cares of a troubled world are made more bearable by the charm of music. Anna Voigt Curtis, front row holding a bouquet, and her husband, Elwood Curtis, D.D.S., back row at the left, founded and

directed this group. They opened their home and grounds each week for rehearsals. They raised funds for numerous worthy causes, including the book collection at the public library, gifts to local Scout groups, and the erection of the clock tower at the high school dedicated to the memory of the town's WW I dead.

The high school band moves north on Broadway with bandmaster Norman Seip, left. This 1945 photograph offers an excellent view of downtown Hicksville 25 years before the New York State Highway Department obliterated four west side blocks of stores and apartments to widen Broadway's Route 107. (Bowman & Brown, Local History Room/HPL.)

Beatlemania and the counterculture of the 1960s rock the social life of Hicksville and Long Island. Young people wait for the Hicksville Theater to open so they can see the Beatles in *A Hard Day's Night*.

Founded in Hicksville, the Singing Boys of Long Island, under Gerald Barker of the Hicksville public school music faculty, successfully emulated the world-renowned Viennese Boys Choir. The Long Island group sang for the pope and at many other occasions of note. (Local History Room/HPL.)

A marching band with a "street beat" that delighted veterans posts on parade are the American Legion Bellaires, Charles Wagner Post 421. Keeping in step was easy, with Peter Seitz's glockenspiel and drum corps youngsters. Seen here, from left to right, are the following: (front row) Steven Hughes, Charlie Petrie, Jimmy Sutton, Kenny Seitz, Jimmy O'Connor, Richie Leger, and Tommy Mangels; (back row) Doreen Weaver, Joe Ratto, Kenny Hirsch, Billy Mangels, Pete Seitz, Kevin Evers, Donald Hughes, and Judy Bosch. (Local History Room/HPL.)

Polish-American youths entertain with traditional folk dances during the Hicksville 325th Anniversary program. Sponsored by the Hicksville Gregory Museum, the three-day program included ethnic recollections. (HGM, Local History Room/HPL.)

In 1965, during the days when Hicksville Junior High School had the largest school population (3,300) under one roof in New York State, the school's 90-piece marching band was led by nationally acclaimed bandmaster Henry Gates, far left. (Local History Room/HPL.)

During the 1960s, these holiday carolers were sponsored by the Rotary International, Kiwanis, and Lions Clubs. At the time, the community Christmas tree was decorated in what is today's Kennedy Memorial Park. (Local History Room/HPL.)

The Holy Family Players rang down their final curtain in 1985, after 20 wonderful years of entertaining Hicksville and neighboring communities. Their nostalgic, family-oriented song-and-dance shows will never be forgotten by those who saw and heard them in the Holy Family Church parish hall, at Octoberfests of Holy Trinity High School, at Hicksville Community Council meetings, during the bicentennial programs of 1976 to 1977, or while residents at area nursing homes.

Listeners experience a rapt moment at the performance of Peter Tarsoly and his Hicksville Middle School String Ensemble during an annual midwinter meeting of the Hicksville Historical Society. The scene is at the Hicksville Gregory Museum in the mid-1990s; attentive young cellist Nicole Metakis is in awe of the older students' music.

Eight

LIVING HISTORY: MONUMENTS AND PAGEANTRY

Historical commemorations and monument dedications are a notable part of Hicksville's life. When the village is not making history, it enjoys remembering and drawing strength from its ceremonial recall of important events. Local history is an absorbing concern of the Hicksville Public Library, the Hicksville Gregory Museum, and the Hicksville Historical Society.

The community has six war memorials recalling the nearly 40 of its brave sons who lost their lives during the great wars of the past century. This WW I Monument shows the names of three Hicksville soldiers who died in France. The glacial boulder and bronze plaque was erected on North Broadway in 1919. The familiar memorial was relocated in 1947 to stand at the high school with the WW II Monument. (Local History Room/HPL.)

The dedication of the WW I Monument took place in 1919 on West Broadway, just north of the Long Island Rail Road. Honored guests included Rev. Lawrence Fuchs, pastor of St. Ignatius Church, and Frank Chlumsky, standing on the dais. This was a day of pride and prayer for "a war to end all wars." The Grand Central Hotel in the background was a landmark until the late 1920s. (Local History Room/HPL.)

The Korean and Vietnam War Memorials were dedicated on Veteran's Day of 1986. Viewing the Vietnam Memorial are Monument Committee Chairman Conrad Steers, Hempstead Town Presiding Supervisor Thomas Gulotta, New York State Assemblyman Fred Parola, and a group of Vietnam veterans who attended the November 11, 1986 program and dedication. (Edward Bady, HGM, Local History Room/HPL.)

On May 15, 1965, a group of Hicksville High School students, led by Latin teacher Samuel Goldberg, were successful in obtaining a stone sculpture that had graced one of the facades of the Pennsylvania Railroad Terminal in New York City for 56 years. With the help of the Long Island Rail Road and the school, the Roman Eagle was transferred to the Hicksville station when the terminal was being demolished to make room for the new Madison Square Garden. Goldberg saw the eagle as a symbol of hope. Although he is no longer with us, "Mr. Goldberg's Eagle" is still at Hicksville today to serve as a reminder to students that they should strive to achieve higher purposes in life. The eagle is indeed a proud symbol to both the Long Island Rail Road and the community.

A parade *c.* 1910 shows the Huettner store in the background and boys gleefully following the band in what may be a Decoration Day celebration.

The centennial of the coming of the railroad to Hicksville was one of the earliest commemorations of Hicksville's history. During a grand parade, high school students dressed as Native Americans recall Hicksville's origins in a land purchase with the Matinecock tribe. Pictured at the far right is Dr. Walter Stillger Jr. (Joseph Burt, Local History Room/HPL.)

The Hicksville Tercentennial, which celebrated the community's 300 years of history, is sometimes called the "turning point." The celebration marks the end of the earlier years of Hicksville and ushers in the great developments that followed. Town crier Donald Smatlak, on horseback, calls together the citizens of the community at the courthouse (today's Hicksville Gregory Museum) to open the tercentennial festivities on May 15, 1948. On the porch in costume are County Historian Jesse Merritt; Bernard Braun; Edna Kuhne Sutton; Gertrude Wetterauer, chair of the commemoration; Lillian Kreider; Sarah Huettner; and Fred Noeth, editor. (Local History Room/HPL.)

These were among the young participants in the 1936 Railroad Centennial Parade. The boy on the pony reminds us that Hicksville then was still a largely rural community. The children in front with the dog portray changes in transportation. (HGM, Local History Room/HPL.)

Young soldiers home from 1991 Persian Gulf War are honored by Hicksville's Desert Shield-Desert Storm program supporters with a rousing parade and ceremony at John F. Kennedy Memorial Park. A number of Hicksville service people participated in the Gulf War. The parade started at the Hicksville Veterans of Foreign Wars Post and continued down to the park, where the rally took place. The turnout and support was tremendous. Many organizations and public officials were present, along with a fine contingent of U.S. Marines; most importantly, the Hicksville community gave the soldiers a heartwarming reception.

The dedication of the new flagpole and national colors at the Jones Institute Home for Elderly People was held *c.* the fall of 1965. Among those taking part were members of the Charles Wagner Post 421 American Legion, the post Color Guard Detachment and Bellaires Band and Color Guard, donor and ceremonial group commander George Johnson, and master of ceremonies Richard Evers. (Local History Room/HPL.)

Frank Mallett photographed this close-up of the excited reception party awaiting the first elevated train's arrival in 1964. Local leaders present are T. Goodfellow, president of the Long Island Rail Road; J. Burns, New York State representative; H. Brodbeck, Civil Defense; and editor Fred Noeth. Jim Cummings can be seen in front of U.S. flag. The costumed young women are students from a local school. (HGM, Local History Room/HPL.)

Proud of their long family heritage in Hicksville are the Steinerts and the Kastens. Standing at the left are Albert Steinert, in the top hat, and Frederick G. Kasten. Seated in the old Ford, which was resurrected from a barn for the celebration, are, from left to right, David Steinert, Edward H. Kasten, Edward D. Kasten Jr., and Freida (Fredericka) Kasten. The Kastens operated a general store at the corner of West Marie Street and Newbridge Road. (Local History Room/HPL.)

The Grand March of the Hicksville Bicentennial Ball of 1976 is under way at the old school hall of St. Ignatius Church. The three bicentennial cochairmen lead off. Present are Siegfried and Iris Widder, Richard and Anne Evers, and Jack Landress and his wife. (Robert Berkowitz, Local History Room/HPL.)

An "Old Time Schoolroom" was the Hicksville Public Library's float in the bicentennial parade. With their "teacher," Donna M., are Stephen Olafsen, Catherine Hundt, Jennifer Olafsen, and Billy Hundt. (Robert Berkowitz, Local History Room/HPL.)

Typically, Hicksville chose to celebrate its 350th anniversary in a yearlong celebration. A climaxing event in September 1998 was the grand community parade, fireworks, and entertainment at the Broadway Mall. As the parade kicks off, Nassau County Executive Thomas Gulotta congratulates Commemoration Cochairmen Karl Schweitzer and Richard Evers. Other dignitaries included Fanny Corsentino, Town of Oyster Bay clerk; Town Councilmen Thomas Clark and Leonard Symons; Edward Mangano, Nassau County legislator; New York State Sen. Carl Marcellino; New York State Assemblyman Marc Herbst; and Town of Oyster Bay Historian and Bicentennial Historical Commissioner Dorothy Horton McGee. (Nassau County photograph.)